A KID'S GUIDE TO FEELINGS

FEELING AFRAID

BY KIRSTY HOLMES

KidHaven
PUBLISHING

Published in 2019 by KidHaven Publishing, an Imprint of Greenhaven Publishing, LLC
353 3rd Avenue, Suite 255, New York, NY 10010

Written by: Kirsty Holmes
Edited by: Holly Duhig
Designed by: Danielle Rippengill

Cataloging-in-Publication Data

Names: Holmes, Kirsty.
Title: Feeling afraid / Kirsty Holmes.
Description: New York : KidHaven Publishing, 2019. | Series: A kid's guide to feelings | Includes glossary and index.
Identifiers: ISBN 9781534526846 (pbk.) | ISBN 9781534526839 (library bound) | ISBN 9781534526853 (6 pack)
Subjects: LCSH: Fear in children--Juvenile literature. | Fear--Juvenile literature. | Emotions--Juvenile literature.
Classification: LCC BF723.F4 H645 2019 | DDC 155.4'1246--dc23

Image Credits: All images are courtesy of Shutterstock.com, unless otherwise specified. With thanks to Getty Images,
Thinkstock Photo and iStockphoto. Front Cover – MarinaMay, pedalist, eurobanks, iconogenic, Yuliya Evstratenko, Armation,
SFerdon, Elnour, yayasya, jirawat phueksriphan, Piotr Urakau. Images used on every page – MarinaMay, yayasya, Piotr Urakau.
4 – jirawat phueksriphan. 5&6 – Andrii Spy_k. 6 – Sudowoodo, Frame Studio, Miuky. 7 – Elnour, Armation. 8 – Olga Sapegina,
wavebreakmedia, pedalist, Vector Tradition SM. 9 – anna.danilkova, joloe, Africa Studio. 11 – FARBAI, Dean Drobot, Littlekidmoment.
12 – DECTER, Cattallina, karelnoppe, iconogenic. 13 – GoodStudio, Romashechka. 14 – Elnour, Armation, Sira Anamwong, LynxVector,
mers1na, Sudowoodo. 15 – sirikorn thamniyom, Africa Studio, ViChizh. 16 – Lucia Fox, Makc, aksenova_yu, Aleksandar Levai.
17 – Anetlanda, FARBAI. 18 – mers1na, nnnnae, Iconic Bestiary, Glinskaja Olga. 19 – Elnour, Armation. 21 – George Rudy,
VectorsMarket, FARBAI. 22 – Andrii Spy_k, Sudowoodo, Miuky. 23 – VectorsMarket, Iconic Bestiary, Glinskaja Olga, Sudowoodo.

Printed in the United States of America

CPSIA compliance information: Batch # BS18KL: For further information contact Greenhaven Publishing LLC, New York, New York at 1-844-317-7404.

CONTENTS

Words that look like **this** can be found in the glossary on page 24.

We all have **emotions**, or feelings, all the time. Our feelings are very important. They help us think about the world around us, and know how we want to **react**.

Sometimes, we feel good. Other times, we feel bad.

Everyone else is ready for bed… but our hero is feeling too afraid!

HOW DO WE FEEL WHEN WE'RE AFRAID?

Your heart might beat really hard...

your body might shake...

you might feel like you have a trembling in your belly...

...or you might want to run away, or cry.

HOW DO WE LOOK
WHEN WE'RE AFRAID?

WIDE EYES!

RAISED EYEBROWS!

SHAKING!

BITTEN NAILS!

OPEN MOUTH!

You can tell someone is afraid because they might…

EEEK!

make a noise…

or cry…

This is called **body language**.

…or they might run away from what is scaring them.

11

WHY DO WE FEEL AFRAID?

FEELING AFRAID IS AN IMPORTANT EMOTION.

Thousands of years ago, humans lived in caves.

Lots of things were dangerous...

FIGHT

SHOUT

RUN

HIDE

...so people **evolved** fear.

12

You might feel afraid if someone is mean to you…

HEY!

…or if you are alone.

OH NO!

We can feel afraid of things that are real, and things that are not.

EEEK!

WHEN FEELING AFRAID IS GOOD

Feeling afraid can be a good thing. If people feel afraid of something real or dangerous, they will know to **avoid** it.

Sometimes we learn what to be afraid of from other people, like our families. This helps us to find out what is safe, and what is not.

It's important to know when we should listen to our feelings of being afraid, and when we should try to find out a little bit more.

It's not nice to feel afraid all the time.

19

Take a deep breath.

GET A FRIEND TO HOLD YOUR HAND!

Ask someone you trust to help you.

FIND OUT MORE ABOUT WHAT IS SCARING YOU.

Confront your fears slowly.

LET'S HELP!

Talking about your feelings can help you to understand why you feel afraid.

GLOSSARY

AVOID	to keep away from something
BODY LANGUAGE	things a person does with their body that tell you how they feel
CONFRONT	to boldly meet, face, or stand up to something scary
EMOTIONS	strong feelings such as joy, hate, sadness, or fear
EVOLVED	developed over a long time to become adapted to a certain habitat
RAISED	lifted up
REACT	act or respond to something that has been done
SURVIVE	continue to live
THREATS	things that can harm you

INDEX